Little book of
Ponies

BBC

Little Book of Ponies

First published in 1999
by BBC Worldwide Ltd
80 Wood Lane, London W12 0TT

ISBN 0 563 55602 1

Colour Reproduction by
Dot Gradations Limited, Wickford
Printed and bound in Italy

Contents

A to Z of

Having trouble thinking of a name for your new pony? Have a look at some of our suggestions!

A Albany, Arab Dancer, Arrow, Art
B Baron, Blossom, Bambie, Bonnie
C Chester, Cassie, Chloe, Chase
D Dawn, Daisy, Dalai, Deedee
E Elsa, Earth, Elijah, Everlasting
F Frosty, Faust, Freddie, Fawn
G Gabriel, Grace, Gretel, Gallop
H Humphrey, Harriet, Hansel, Hattie
I Icarus, Isis, Isaac, Ickle
J Juno, Jez, Jupiter, Jojo
K King Lear, Kilkenny, Kenya, Kayley

Pony Names

L Lola, Lancelot, Laughter, Love
M Mercury, Mistletoe, Moon, Magic
N Neptune, Napoleon, Naples, Nice
O Otto, Oswald, Orinocho, Oregon
P Primrose, Pegasus, Perky, Pepper
Q Quarrel, Quixote, Quebec, Quartz
R Romany, Roly, Roschine, Rigby
S Spy, Smiffie, Scarlet, Sammy
T Trumpet, Telly, Tobias, Thai
U Urchin, Unity, Urgent, Uffy
V Venus, Verdi, Verve, Valhalla
W Willow, Whisky, Wolfgang, Whisper
X Xmas, Xhosas, Xion, Xanthy
Y Yazoo, Yuppy, Yumyum, Yoyo
Z Zola, Zippy, Zulu, Zara

THINK

BEFORE YOU GET A PONY!

ALTERNATIVES TO OWNING A PONY

Having a pony or horse is wonderful, but owning one is a great responsibility and there are many alternatives to buying your own pony.

There are plenty of places to go and see ponies and horses in action:

1. Horse races and point-to-points
2. Gymkhanas
3. Eventing competitions
4. Polo matches
5. Rescue centres
6. Local stables

You can also volunteer to help at some places, or perhaps you could ask a friend if you could help with the care and exercise of their horse. Of course, the most obvious alternative to owning a pony is to join ▶

THINK BEFORE YOU GET A PONY!

a local riding school. Particularly if you are a novice rider, you should never consider taking on a pony until you are capable of looking after one.

BEFORE YOU GET A PONY, ASK...

● Are you prepared to commit yourself to looking after it for the whole of its life?

● Do you have the time and patience needed to care for it? Remember, a pony needs exercise and grooming every day, regular feeds, and, if kept in a stable, a lot of mucking out and other maintenance.

● Could you ensure that your pony received a balanced diet?

● Are you able to give your pony enough physical and mental exercise?

● Are you prepared to be responsible for your pony's healthcare which could include vaccinations, worming, dental care, grooming and even surgery?

● Can you afford the expense of your pony's food, equipment and healthcare, especially if it gets sick

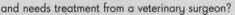

and needs treatment from a veterinary surgeon?

- Where will you keep your pony?
- Who will look after your pony when you go away on holiday?
- Do you know a good farrier who will look after your pony's feet properly and a local vet who will check on your pony's health regularly?
- What sort of pony or horse will suit you best? If you are disabled, nervous or a novice rider, you will want a docile, well-schooled and experienced pony.
- What do you want the pony for: general hacking, racing, dressage, jumping or competition work?
- Would you prefer a male or female?
- Where will you get your pony from?
- Do you have any other pets, particularly other ponies or horses? How will they react to the new arrival? Can you see any potential problems?
- What about the rest of your family? Having a pony will also affect them, especially because of the expense and demands on their time.

PONY

Albino Pony or horse has pure white hair, pale skin and pale, translucent eyes.

Black Pony has black coat, mane and tail with no other colour present except possibly white markings on the face and/or legs.

Cream or Cremello Horse has cream-coloured coat.

Dun Yellow, blue, sandy or mouse-coloured coat.

COLOURS

Grey Dark-skinned horse with a coat of mixed black and white hairs; the whiter hairs become more dominant as the horse ages.

Piebald Irregular, large patches of white and black.

Palomino Golden coat, white mane and tail, sometimes with a small amount of black.

Bay Dark-skinned horse with a coat ranging from dark brown to bright reddish or yellow-brown in colour, black mane and tail and usually black markings on legs.

Chestnut Gold to dark reddish-brown coated pony, usually having a matching or slightly lighter or darker mane and tail, or with a flaxen-coloured mane and tail.

Roan Pony has a black, chestnut or bay coat with a mixture of white hairs, especially on the body and neck, which changes the colour slightly.

Skewbald The pony's coat is a mixture of large irregular and clearly-defined patches of white and any other colour except black.

Spotted Small, more or less circular patches of hair which are different from the main colour of the coat and are distributed widely across the coat.

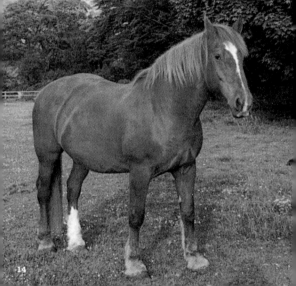

PONY MARKINGS

14

Here are some examples of the most common forms of markings which occur as patches of white hairs on the face and legs.

STAR Small, white patch on top of the face.

STRIPE A thin stripe of white hairs from the top of the nose down towards the horse's mouth.

WHITE MUZZLE White patch around the horse's mouth and nostrils.

WHITE LIPS The horse has white hair around the lips/mouth only.

BLAZE A thick band of white hairs down the face and covering the muzzle but not around the eyes.

SNIP A small patch of isolated white hairs on the nose between the nostrils.

WHITE FACE The horse has white hairs covering the forehead and over the eyes and the front of the face and extending out towards the mouth, and possibly also covering the muzzle and lower ear.

INTERRUPTED STRIPE A stripe of white hairs down the horse's nose with a gap or break in the middle where the coat's normal colour is seen.

SOCK White patch of colouring anywhere up to the horse's knee.

STOCKING White colouring covering the knee.

NAME THAT

There are many equestrian terms that people use daily to describe a horse, without necessarily knowing what they really mean. So here is a quick list of horse terms to start you off on the right foot!

BRONCO An unbroken or imperfectly broken horse.
COB A short-legged horse with a top height of 15 hands, with the stature of a heavyweight hunter and capable of carrying a substantial weight.

HORSE!

COLT An ungelded male horse of less than four years old.

DAM The mother of a foal.

FILLY A female horse less than four years old.

FOAL A young horse up to the age of 12 months.

GELDING A male horse which has been castrated.

GREEN A horse which is broken but not fully trained; an inexperienced horse.

HACK A lightly-built horse not more than 15 hands.

HORSE The general term for a stallion, mare or gelding.

MARE A female horse aged four years or over.

MUSTANG A wild horse.

PONY A horse shorter than 14 hands, 2 inches at maturity.

STALLION An ungelded male horse aged four years or over.

CHOOSING

Choosing the right pony to suit you and your needs is of utmost importance, not only because a pony can be extremely expensive but because you will play a crucial role in each other's daily lives. Here are a few common sense tips to choosing the right pony:

1. Never buy a pony without seeing and trying it yourself.
2. Always take an expert along or someone who has much experience with horses.
3. Ask lots of questions. For example, does it allow itself to be caught easily? Is it well-mannered in the stable? What is its normal daily routine? What is the pony fed?
4. Watch how the pony behaves when being tacked.
5. Check out the pony's body to make sure there are no unusual lumps or evidence of injuries.
6. Watch the horse being led up towards you, turned and walked away by the current owner.
7. Ask the owner to walk and trot the pony on a loose rein, both away from and towards you.

YOUR PONY

8. Check how the pony reacts to being ridden by a familiar rider, then ask your expert to put the pony through its paces, particularly if the owner failed to ask the pony to do certain things.

9. Have a look at its stable for signs of behavioural problems; are there any kick marks or signs of chewing?

10. Watch for clues to its personality (see pages 26 to 31). Does the owner seem to have any problems handling the pony?

11. How does the horse behave in all sorts of traffic (not just cars) and on roads?

12. How does the horse react to the presence of other people, horses and dogs?

13. Can you provide a certain amount of continuity to its habitat? Is the horse used to being stabled or kept in open pasture, or a combination of both?

14. Ride the pony yourself to determine if it is suitable for your style of riding.

15. Only buy the pony subject to an 'all-clear' examination and certificate from your chosen vet.

WELCOME HOME PONY

11 WAYS TO MAKE YOUR PONY FEEL AT HOME

1. Reassure your pony by talking softly to it.

2. Water and feed your pony and give it an extra food treat, such as an apple.

3. Give your pony a good groom. This physical contact should help you to bond with your pony.

4. If an object startles your pony, give it time to smell the object so it can learn not to be afraid of it.

5. Allow your pony to explore its stable and bed and generally get the feel of its new home before introducing it to new people and/or places.

6. Exercise your pony as soon as possible and encourage your pony with confidence when riding.

7. As horses get bored easily and are essentially 'herd' animals, they prefer company. Introduce your horse to some of 'its own kind' to help put it at ease.

8. To prevent bullying, introduce the pony to a member of the 'herd' and exercise them together before allowing the new pony to share pasture.

9. In winter and cold weather, make sure stabled horses have rugs and bedding to keep them warm.

10. Pat your pony's head, ears, and body.

11. Keep to a routine to make your pony feel secure about when it will see you each day.

Your Pony's

Tack, or saddlery, is essential equipment that helps training and ensures a comfortable, controlled and safe ride when fitted and used properly.

There are lots of different pieces of tack but the minimum needed is a saddle and bridle.

BRIDLE
Made up of a headpiece, browband, noseband, reins and adjustable cheekpieces. The bit is attached to the bridle, which is usually leather.

SNAFFLE
A type of bit.

BREASTPLATE
Prevents the saddle from slipping back.

STIRRUP IRONS
Made of stainless steel and attached to good quality leather stirrup straps.

GIRTH
Strap attached to the saddle, made of leather, cotton, wool, web or nylon. Steel buckles are used.

Tack

NUMNAH A soft saddle pad fitted under the saddle to give greater comfort to the horse's back.

THE SADDLE

Different types of saddle are used for each type of activity:

DRESSAGE A deeper seat with long saddle flaps.

RACING Lightweight to allow the best forward position possible.

SHOW A flat seat and straight-cut flaps to show off the horse's shoulders.

LONG DISTANCE A deep and resilient panel, with a fairly broad-waisted seat and extra padding for comfort.

JUMPING Deep-seated with forward-set saddle flaps and padded knee rolls.

PONY'S

A pony or horse will need a balanced diet and daily exercise to keep it fit and healthy. A daily routine of care and maintenance will help keep your animal happy and healthy. Watch its body language for signs of ill-health or behavioural problems and signals that there is something wrong. (See pages 26 to 31)

● A healthy horse or pony has an alert look with pricked ears and clear, bright eyes.

HEALTH

● Its coat should be shiny. The skin should move freely over the underlying tissue. There should be no bare patches of skin, which could indicate lice or ringworm.

● The horse's limbs should be cool to the touch as a warm spot indicates a problem. They should be free from swelling, wounds or sores of any kind.

● You can also help to keep your pony healthy by maintaining a safe environment. Its stable should be clean and tidy and its pasture is another area which needs to be checked for the presence of poisonous plants, trees and shrubs.

● Plants, trees and shrubs which are poisonous to horses (in different quantities) include: acorns, box, bracken, buttercup, foxglove, hemlock, horsetail, laurel, oleander, privet, ragwort, rhododendron, yellow star thistle and yew.

HORSE

How does a horse express itself and how does it communicate with other horses and humans?

SOUNDS

● **Squeals** and **grunts** are usually signs of aggression, excitement or recognition.

● **Snorts** indicate the horse has seen or smelled something that is interesting or potentially dangerous.

● Horses **neigh** or **whinny** to companions and humans. They do this out of affection, excitement or when seeking attention.

● A mare will **whicker** or **nicker** softly to reassure her foal or to tell it to 'Come closer'. It is nearly always a friendly 'Hello' or 'Come here' sound and so is used as a greeting between horses.

● When horses are having a serious fight they may **roar** or even **scream** out of intense rage or fear, and sometimes both. This sound is rarely heard in domestic horses.

TALK

BODY LANGUAGE:
- ### EARS

A horse's ears are extremely expressive, but don't forget that in the course of a typical day, the ears will react according to their main function, hearing. One of the most powerful signs of aggression in a horse is when its ears are pinned back. A horse will pin its ears back so that they do not become torn or bitten in a potential fight. A horse with its ears pinned back might be saying, 'Don't come any closer or I will bite you'.

When the ears are erect, twitching and flicking, the horse is likely to be scared stiff and may well be on the verge of bolting in terror. This is an extension of pricked ears.

A horse will prick up its ▶

ears when it is startled, watchful, alert, interested and also when it is greeting a companion. The opposite of this is 'airplane ears'. This is when they flop out to the side with their openings faced down. Airplane ears signify a tired, lethargic or disinterested horse.

● BODY

In general, the more elevated a horse's posture, the more excited the horse is likely to be. The head is held high and the tail stands up proudly. In contrast, a slumped posture and a drooping tail indicate a drowsy, bored or sleepy animal.

Horses can also use their bodies to 'bully' other horses by body-checking, shoulder-barging and presenting their rumps to each other. The body-check and more forceful shoulder-barge are used to remind other horses who is 'in charge'. When a horse presents its rump to another horse, it is a defensive, more guarded form of threat, like, 'If you don't stop that, I'll rear-kick you'.

● TAIL

A horse's tail acts like an excitement indicator. When the tail is high it indicates joy and alertness. When it droops down the horse may be tired, in pain, afraid or submissive.

If a horse is very tense or aggressive, it may stiffen the fleshy part of its tail so that it sticks out away from the horse more than usual.

A swishing tail indicates irritation, anxiety or confusion and if it begins to swish more violently, the horse may be angry and it might give a brutal kick.

● NECK

When a horse moves its neck from side to side or up and down in a head shake, upward head toss or jerk, it is usually a signal of irritation and annoyance, ▶

as though it is being hassled by flies or insects. It may do this whether its 'irritant' is human or another horse.

Forward head movements like head-thrusting, lungeing and nose-nudging are all self-assertive actions, although a nudge is not necessarily aggressive, more of a demand for attention. Sometimes this nudge is used to get attention when a horse is in pain or acute discomfort.

When a horse signals that it is trying to avoid something, it swings its head away from the source of unpleasantness. A quick twist of the neck may also show that the horse finds something distasteful.

● LEGS

There are several leg signals used by horses: knocking, stamping and leg-lifts. Most of the time, these signals indicate frustration, annoyance or increasing irritation or anger. A horse may paw the ground to indicate its desire to go forward when it is not able to do so, for example, when a fear or

physical
obstacle
prevents
its
advance.

● **FACE**

A horse's
face can tell
you a lot about
its mood. A
horse can, for example,
wrinkle up its nostrils in disgust or flare its nostrils
when in a state of intense emotion or excitement.
Similarly, when a horse is content, submissive or
peacefully relaxed it may well have half-closed eyes,
whereas wide open eyes indicate fear and anxiety.
Angry eyes look back and show some white, but not
every horse that has some white showing is hostile. It
may just have caught a glimpse of something behind
that is particularly interesting.

31

SADDLE

It is very important to fit a saddle properly to prevent the withers from being pinched or the pony's back from being damaged by pressure on its spine. The saddle should also not affect the action of the shoulders. The saddle is held in place by the 'girth', traditionally made of leather but also available in synthetic materials.

The right way to fit a saddle

1. Place the saddle gently over the withers a little farther forward than its final position so that you can push it back, ensuring that the hairs lie flat beneath.
2. Attach the girth to the straps under the saddle flap on the off (right hand) side before bringing it under the pony's tummy. Don't attempt to fully tighten it when first fitted – wait a few minutes and then tighten the girth to keep the saddle in place.
3. Fasten the girth on the near side. The saddle should not be able to rock around on the pony's

back, nor should it be so tight-fitting that it hurts your pony.

4. As most horses and ponies tend to 'blow themselves out' when being girthed, wait a few minutes and then check the fit again.

SADDLERY CARE
Practical Advice

Leather tack must be properly protected from water, heat and wear-and-tear or it will become brittle and crack, and this could be very dangerous.

Tack should be cleaned frequently, at least every other day (depending on usage and conditions of its use) and should be inspected regularly for signs of undue wear and loose stitching.

1. Remove any sweat, grease and mud deposits which will clog the pores of the leather with a sponge dampened in lukewarm water.

2. Use a chamois cloth to remove any surplus water before allowing the leather to dry naturally.

3. Using a different, slightly damp sponge, rub saddle soap into the leather to condition and nourish the leather.

4. Finally, polish the leather with a chamois cloth to give the leather a supple feel and a sheen.

5. Metal parts can be washed and treated with a special metal cleaner, except for the mouthpiece of the bit.

CLOTHES

Safety is vital when working with horses. Dark clothes are practical, while competitions have a dress code.

1. Hard hat: fastened and well-fitting to protect your head in case of falls.
2. Gloves
3. Never wear jewellery!
4. Long hair should be tied up.
5. Sturdy wellingtons or leather jodhpur boots. Trainers are no protection against a horse's weight!
6. Comfortable, well-fitting trousers, jeans or jodhpurs. Tight clothes are not suitable for bending.
7. Long-sleeved shirt, jumper or sweatshirt to protect you in case you are nipped or bitten.
8. Jackets or body-warmers should be fastened. A flapping coat might startle a nervous horse.
9. If you have poor eyesight, soft contact lenses are the safest option but if it is not possible, the optician will be able to advise you on the safest glasses.
10. If you ride in poor light or on the roads, always wear reflective, fluorescent vests or bands.

HORSE

DOCK

LOINS

FLANK

TAIL

GASKIN

HOCK

HIND LEG

ANATOMY

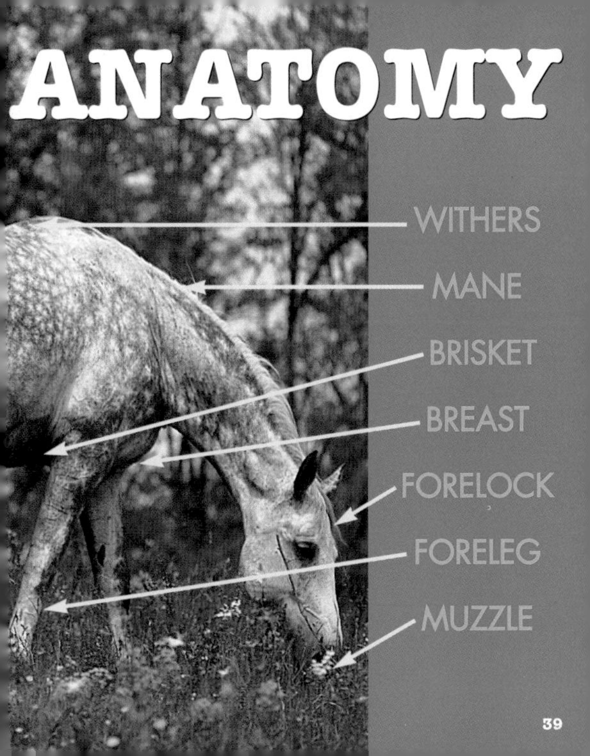

WITHERS

MANE

BRISKET

BREAST

FORELOCK

FORELEG

MUZZLE

The horse family has been around for millions of years and, on this time scale, was domesticated by man only fairly recently: around 6,000 years ago!

The original horse was only about the size of a hare, had a long tail, a curved back and had four toes on the front and three on the back, totally unlike the horse we know today.

Right from the start, apart from being kept for food, horses have been bred for either speed or strength. They have been used for thousands of years to carry both man and heavy goods.

Horses are an essential part of our history, particularly because of their role in warfare. Many important battles have been won and lost because of the speed, size and endurance of horses. ▶

PONIES IN HISTORY

Once domesticated enough to work in partnership with man, horse and chariots were replaced by strong, heavy horses which carried heavily-armoured soldiers, which in turn were replaced by light cavalry. These lighter, faster horses are still used today.

In Britain, horses had their heyday in Victorian times. Horses were used for drawing buses, cabs, trams and barges and, because horses were considered more reliable, fought off competition from motorised vehicles for many years. Horses were also used for agricultural work, such as pulling ploughs.

'Vestry horses', used to move rubbish, were chosen for their ability to carry heavy loads and manoeuvre around tight corners and narrow paths.

Breweries used horses to transport their heavy barrels. Ponies, because of their size, sure-footedness and strength, were employed in coal pits for many years.

But it is not just the horse's employment possibilities that kept it popular. Horses have long been part of sport and entertainment. Ancient Greek vases depict chariot races and hunting.

Today, there are still many different categories of horse and pony sports, including flat racing, dressage, jumping and steeplechasing, and the horse is valued as a beautiful, intelligent and skilled animal.

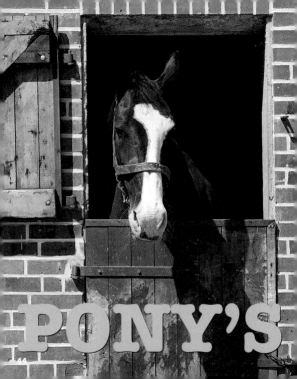

THE STABLE SHOULD BE:

1. Warm
2. Dry
3. Free from draughts and sheltered
4. Clean
5. Comfortable
6. Relaxing
7. Large enough for horse to lie down/roll over
8. High enough so that if the horse rears it won't be injured
9. Well-ventilated
10. Safe

It should also have good drainage, plenty of suitable bedding (more during winter, in old age, sickness or foaling) and a view of surroundings to keep the pony interested in its environment and what's going on in the yard. ▶

HOME

PONY'S HOME

HERE ARE THE
BASIC TOOLS
NEEDED TO
MAKE YOUR
PONY'S HOME
CLEAN AND COSY:

- Rake
- Shovel
- Wheelbarrow
- Four-pronged fork
- Broom
- Muck skip (or similar object to collect droppings)
- Bedding (straw, shavings or shredded paper)
- Disinfectant
- Wellingtons

GOLDEN RULES
- Muck out daily
- Make sure there is plenty of fresh, clean drinking

water available
- Feed should be little and often
- Bedding should be kept fresh, clean and free from trodden-in muck.

DID YOU KNOW...
Horses and ponies tend to do their droppings in the same place in the stable each day.

47

RECORD-BREAKING

OLDEST HORSE

The oldest horse recorded was 62 years old. His name was 'Old Billy', and he worked towing barges on a canal in Lancashire. He was born in 1760 and died in 1822.

OLDEST PONY

The oldest pony recorded was a stallion who lived in Central France. He died in 1919 at the grand age of 54 years.

GRAND NATIONAL WINNER

In 1973, Red Rum completed the 4.5 mile long Grand National race in nine minutes, 1.9 seconds.

LONGEST HORSE RACE

The longest horse race in history was probably one in Portugal which was over 1,200 miles long. The race was won by 'Emir', an Egyptian-bred Arab horse.

WALK TALL

One of the tallest horses ever recorded was 'Dr Le Gear', a Percheron. Born in 1902, it stood 21 hands at the withers and weighed 1,370kg.

48

HORSE FEATS

EYE SPY
Not only do horses have excellent eyesight, but they also have the largest eye of all land mammals.

FIRST STEEPLECHASE
The first steeplechase was held in Ireland in 1752. It was held between two men, Mr O'Callaghan and Mr Blake, over a distance of 4.5 miles, measured from one church steeple to another.

WALK SMALL
In 1969, a Shetland Pony called 'Midnight' was said to have been only 36cm tall.

LONG JUMP
One of the longest jumps recorded was that of Colonel Lopez del Hierro with his horse 'Amado' in November 1951. It is reputed that they jumped 8.3 metres.

MOST EXPENSIVE DRAFT HORSE
In 1911 a Scotsman bought 'Baron of Buchlyvie', a Clydesdale stallion, for a sum of £9,500, which was a vast amount of money in those days.

49

COLIC
Colic is a digestive disorder
SIGNS

Its symptoms include severe abdominal pain which might make the animal stand and look round at or try to kick its flank or abdomen. The horse may also sweat, with a temperature of above 39 degrees Celsius. It may also lie down, roll around and get up again, kicking its abdomen.

CAUSE

Poor feeding, sudden change in diet, worm infection, twisted gut, impacted intestines.

TREATMENT

Call the vet if it is very severe or lasts longer than an hour. Remove food and water, increase bedding to prevent injury. If the pony is restless, walk it around gently. In rare cases, surgery is needed. Do not let

ILLNESSES

the pony lie down and do not let the pony roll over as this increases the risk of a twisted gut.

EQUINE INFLUENZA
Horse flu
SIGNS
Appetite loss, exhaustion, shallow cough, high temperature and other, general, cold-like symptoms, such as white or yellow nasal discharge.
CAUSE Viral infection
TREATMENT
Call the vet immediately. Isolate the animal. Keep the pony warm, well-rested and take its temperature regularly. The vet may prescribe antibiotics to help. But PREVENTION BY REGULAR VACCINATIONS is the best way you can help your horse. Contact your veterinary surgeon for details.

WHEN TO

62

CALL THE VET

As you get to know your horse or pony, you will become aware of its condition and behaviour when it is healthy. Here is a guide to indications that something might be wrong. If your pony shows any of these signs, you should watch it carefully for clues to the problem and call the veterinary surgeon.

Signs Of Ill-health
1. Changes in appetite or behaviour
2. Nasal discharge
3. Sore eyes
4. Coughing
5. Dull coat
6. Temperature of 39 degrees Celsius or above
7. Change in consistency or frequency of horse's droppings
8. Lameness
9. Lethargy

Common Illnesses And Conditions:
Azoturia, C.O.P.D, Equine Influenza, Colic, Grass Sickness, Mud Fever, Rain Scald, Ringworm, Strangles, Tetanus, Sweet Itch, Wounds, Laminitis.

GIDDY-UP

The natural movement of humans is limited in many ways, not least because we have only two legs.

Whether we walk, jog or run, the pattern or sequence of footfalls is always the same: left leg, right leg, left leg, right leg, and so on.

This is not the case with horses and ponies.

There are four natural 'gaits' or ways in which a horse moves itself along. These are:

1. WALK

The horse's walk is a regular movement and has four distinct beats. When it starts with the right hind leg, it has the following sequence of footfalls:

1. right hind 2. right fore 3. left hind 4. left fore.

2. TROT

Two distinct beats can be heard when the horse or pony trots, because the horse puts one pair of diagonal legs to the ground at the same time. After a moment of suspension it springs onto the other diagonal pair. The sequence for trotting is:

1. left hind + right fore 2. right hind + left fore.

3. CANTER

The horse's third natural gait, the canter, is a three-beat sequence of movement. When it begins on the right hind, the footfall pattern is as follows:
1. right hind 2. right diagonal, right foreleg and left hind touching the ground at the same time 3. left fore. In this sequence of footfalls, the left fore is referred to as the 'leading leg'.

4. GALLOP

This is the fastest normal 'run' of a horse and is the most exciting, because there is always a period when all four feet are in the air. When the horse gallops very fast, you can't always hear all four beats. The sequence of footfalls varies according to the speed. If the right fore is the leading leg, the pattern of footfalls is:
1. left hind 2. right hind 3. left fore 4. right fore. This is followed by a gap of full suspension.

FROM THE
HORSE'S

● Horses belong to the equus family, hence the terms 'equine' and 'equestrian'. Donkeys, mules and zebra also belong to this group.

● Horses have been around for centuries. There are even caveman pictures of horse-like animals painted on ancient cave walls.

● The first horseshoes were sandals made from grass or reeds. They were used in Asia and the Middle East until the 19th century.

● For centuries, horses have been associated with luck, superstition and religion.

● At one time, white horses were seen as bringing bad luck, while an ancient Arab tribe leader ordered all his pure black Arab horses to be killed because it

MOUTH...

was thought a black horse had brought his men defeat on the battlefield.

● Some people hang horseshoes open side down over a doorway so that the luck spills over all who enter. Others hang up the shoe open side up, so that the luck doesn't run out.

● An average life span for a horse is around 20-25 years, though they can live for 30 years or more.

● Did you know that you really can tell how old a horse is by looking at its teeth? It is fairly accurate in horses up to ten years of age but gets more difficult as the horse gets older.

● In the USA, any style of riding other than the 'Western' style is called 'English'.

Ponies in

the Wild

Semi-wild ponies graze on Dartmoor

One of the most interesting living species of wild horse is the Przewalski Horse, also known as the Asiatic or Mongolian Wild Horse.

The Przewalski horse differs genetically from the domesticated horse, having 66 chromosomes instead of 64.

In appearance, it has several primitive features, such as a large head with the eyes set high up rather than to the side of the head, long ears, thick neck and heavy body.

It is the size of a small pony, standing at about 12 to 13 hands, with a yellowish-brown ▶

Ponies in the Wild

Two piebald Dartmoor ponies pause by the roadside.

coloured coat with a short mane, a dark stripe down its back and zebra markings on the legs.

Przewalski horses are very hardy and can endure extreme heat and cold. They resist all attempts to train them for riding.

Free-ranging horses and ponies exist in various parts of the world.

In Britain, several of the moorland pony breeds like the Dartmoor pony, lead semi-wild lives, as do some of the horses bred in the former USSR. Camargue horses lead a semi-wild existence in southern France.

The North American Mustangs are perhaps the most famous 'wild' horses. Mustangs can be found roaming in small herds.

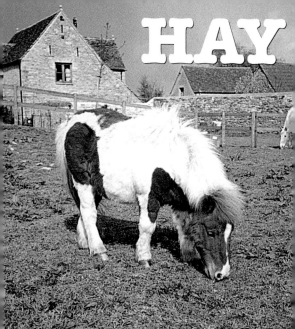

HAY

THERE!

Horses need a varied and balanced diet, just like humans. Horses are strictly herbivores but they need to get all the vitamins and minerals from their food and water, which must always be readily available.

Whatever you feed your horse, make sure that bulk makes up between half and two-thirds of the diet.

Roughage: this includes seed hay (very nutritious), meadow hay and chaff or chop.

Roots and fruit: which add variety to the diet as well as providing necessary minerals and vitamins.

Salt lick or mineral blocks: a valuable source of sodium chloride and minerals which may only be available in limited amounts in natural plants.

Concentrates: including oats, barley, bran, maize, linseed, sugar beet and cod liver oil. Concentrates also come in cube form or as a coarse mix known as compound or general feeds. These are made of a range of scientifically determined ingredients which give a complete, balanced diet, according to the amount of work each horse is doing.

WESTERN RIDING AND RODEOS The skills of a cowboy and his horse are legendary and, while still seen on some ranches, mainly survive at rodeos where competitions include cutting, barrel-racing, bronco-busting and steer-roping events. A cutting horse is one that is used to separate one animal from the rest of the group. It works in a similar way to a sheepdog and needs very little guidance from its rider.

POLICE HORSES Highly-trained horses are used by police forces all over the world, especially for crowd control. The armed forces still use a number of horses. The Royal Tournament, held annually at Earl's Court in London, is a display of the skills of the horse and its rider, working together as a team in the Police, Army and Horse Guards, for example.

OTHER FIELDS IN WHICH PONIES WORK:

1. RACING
2. HUNTING
3. POLO
4. STEEPLECHASING
5. DRESSAGE
6. EVENTING
7. LONG-DISTANCE
8. CATTLE HERDING
9. AGRICULTURE & FORESTRY
10. TOURISM
11. SHOW JUMPING
12. TREKKING

GROOMING

DANDY BRUSH Has long, stiff bristles to remove mud and stable stains

BODY BRUSH Shorter, finer bristles for entire body and legs to remove grease from the coat

METAL CURRY COMB Used to clean brushes after every few strokes

WATER BRUSH For dampening down mane and tail

TWO SPONGES Use one for cleaning eyes and nostrils, the other to clean the dock. Make sure you don't mix them up!

HOOF PICK Cleans out horse's feet

STABLE RUBBER For final polishing of coat, use slightly damp

RUBBER OR PLASTIC CURRY COMB Removes dried mud from coat; removes winter coat when the pony is moulting in the spring

SWEAT SCRAPER Removes excess water after washing down

TRIMMING SCISSORS & MANE COMBS To trim the heels and pull the mane and tail

GUIDE

1. Don't overgroom your pony.

2. Never sit or kneel on the floor to reach the lower parts! Squat or bend so you can react quickly if the horse moves! Never stand directly behind the horse!

3. When grooming, always keep an eye out for skin injuries and lumps or bumps, especially on the legs, which could warn of impending health problems.

4. Use rugs to dry off a wet horse in the stable and to keep a clipped horse warm during grooming.

5. Give all rugs and blankets a thorough shaking every week. It is pointless putting a dusty or dirty rug back onto a clean animal.

6. All equipment should be cleaned regularly.

7. Never groom a sweaty horse! Wait until it is dry.

8. Never try and brush off wet mud! Let it dry first or hose it off with water.

9. Never use a metal curry comb on the horse's body! It is too harsh.

10. Always take care when grooming not to hurt the horse, particularly around bony and sensitive areas.

PONY

There are over 150 different breeds and types of horse in the world. However, a relationship between them all can be traced.

The only pure breed is the Arab, which is unique. In the past couple of centuries, the bigger, faster Thoroughbred has developed from the Arabian horse.

Other breeds have been influenced greatly by the Barb of North Africa and the Andalucian Spanish horse.

The biggest factor influencing the development of horse breeds is man and the type of work which humans required each particular horse to perform.

For example, those who needed horses to move heavy loads bred for strength while those who needed fast transportation bred for speed.

There are also purely man-made breeds which are artificial in character. A typical example of this is the miniature Falabella horse.

Many horses still exist in the wild, such as the

BREEDS

Asiatic wild horse called the 'Przewalski' (see page 59), the 'Tarpan' from eastern Europe and the Australian 'Brumby'.

THE ARAB

CHARACTERISTICS

Height 14-15 hands
Colour Bay, brown, chestnut, grey or black.
Temperament Excellent. Kind, gentle, willing, high-spirited.

Arab stallion cantering gracefully

Use Good all-round riding horse, racing, long-distance riding.
Special features Stamina, endurance. The Arab has 17 ribs while other horses have 18; five lumbar bones (other horses have six) and 16 tail vertebrae (other horses have 18). ▶

THE BARB

CHARACTERISTICS

Height 14.2-15.2 hands
Colour Originally bay, dark bay and black but now also grey.
Temperament Tough, good.
Use As a mount for the fierce North African fighting horsemen and France's famous Spahi cavalry.
Special features Agility, short distance speed, stamina, endurance. Less attractive than the Arab or Andalusian with its primitive skull shape, Roman nose, flat shoulders, short back and low-set tail.
Note Second only to the Arab in terms of being a great influence in the equine world.

THE ANDALUSIAN

CHARACTERISTICS

Height 15-15.2 hands
Colour Bay or shades of grey.
Temperament Excellent. Easy to manage.
Use As a mount for

Andalusian mare and foal

the Spanish bullfighters, dressage, show jumping.
Special features Strength, endurance, natural balance,
agility. Very long and often wavy tail, handsome
head, broad and strong hind quarters.

THE SHETLAND PONY

CHARACTERISTICS

Height 26-44 inches
Colour Black
(main colour),
brown, chestnut,
grey, skewbald
and piebald.
Temperament

Shetland pony

Excellent. Gentle, courageous, easy to manage.
Use Ideal child's pony, riding, driving, used to be
used to pull carts on the Shetlands and were in great
demand for pit work.
Special features Hardiness, strength, endurance. The
Shetland pony has a stocky build, with a short back
and limbs and tough round feet. Its neck is muscular
and strong. It has wide nostrils and a full, thick mane
and tail.

HEIGHT, GIRTH AND OTHER MEASUREMENTS

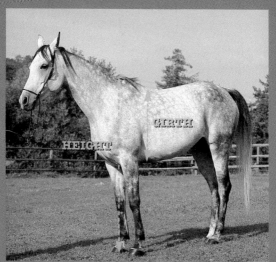

HEIGHT
The height of a horse or pony is measured as the distance from the highest part of the withers down to the ground.

HANDS
The height of a horse or pony is measured in 'hands'. One hand is equal to 10cm.

GIRTH
The 'girth' of a horse or pony is the circumference measured behind the withers round the deepest (fattest) part of the body.

NOSE
The shortest measure of distance by which a horse can win a race.

HEAD
The length of a horse's head. One of the distances by which a horse can win a race.

NECK
The length of a horse's head and neck. Another distance by which a horse can win a race. The phrase 'neck and neck' comes from this.

LENGTH
The length of the horse's head and body; one of the distances by which a horse can win a race.

PONY TAILS

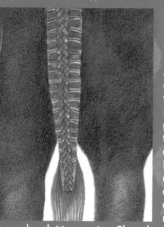

NATURAL TAIL The natural tail is left long and thick.

BANG TAIL A 'banged' tail is cut straight across the bottom to make it look neat and gives a scraggly tail a thicker, fuller appearance.

PULLED TAIL The hair at the top around the dock area is pulled out to give the tail a more refined look and make plaiting easier. Show horses frequently have pulled tails.

PLAITED TAIL The tail is first pulled then plaited around the dock for showing. Both manes and tails are usually plaited for dressage.

74

TIPS FOR TAILS

1. The hair must be clean, damp and well-brushed before you start to plait a horse's tail.
2. Begin high up using one small bunch of hair from each side and one from the centre.
3. Plait down to the end of the dock using thin bunches from alternate sides.
4. At the end of the dock, stop adding side bunches and continue plaiting the long hair in the usual way.
5. The bottom of the plait should be secured with a thick rubber band or needle and thread.
6. Roll the plaited tail up under the dock and carefully sew to hold it in place.

75

ROSETTE

Whether you are running your own informal competition with your riding friends or just rewarding a pony for being so special, our Make It! Rosettes are simple to make and look great!

FOR EACH ROSETTE, YOU WILL NEED:

- 60cm of 4cm-wide ribbon
- Card
- Ruler
- Scissors
- Needle and thread
- A photo of a pony

1. Cut out two circles of card. One should be 4cm across and the other 5cm across. You can use a ruler to measure the correct diameter.

2. Cut the ribbon to one 45cm piece.

3. Fold it into pleats one centimetre across.
4. Stitch each pleat just below the top.
5. When finished, sew the ends together.
6. Open it out and arrange the pleats evenly.
7. Put the rosette down on the large circle and sew it in place with a few large stitches.
8. Cut the remaining ribbon lengthways into two thin strips.
9. Cut a triangle out of one end of each piece.
10. Sew the strips onto the centre of the rosette.
11. Stick a picture of your pony in the middle of the rosette so that it covers the stitches and ribbon.

You can use the leftover card to make yourself a matching badge by sticking a photo of your pony onto the card with glue. Turn over the card and use sticky tape to attach a safety pin so that it is ready to wear.

EXERCISE

You can exercise a pony in many ways. The range of activities and fun games you can do with a horse is endless.

When riding, you can walk, canter, gallop, do sitting and rising trot, learn how to change the leading leg, test and improve the pony's skills and reactions by jumping it using trotting poles.

Suppleness and balance can be improved by doing circles, while individual muscles can be built up by using different exercises. Any type of hillwork, for example, helps build muscle, especially in the pony's hindquarters.

The stabled horse or pony needs daily exercise to keep it healthy and maintain its condition. Extra exercise will obviously help build up its strength and fitness level, which might be desired if your horse is in work or you want it to compete.

If you can, you should turn your stabled horse out to ▶

EXERCISE

grass for part of each day. Not only does this mean that it can exercise itself naturally but the change in scene will help prevent it from developing bad stable habits, such as wood chewing, kicking and weaving.

If you are able to turn out your horse daily, you should still continue its normal exercise routine.

As intelligent animals, variety is the spice of life for both humans and horses. And no-one likes being cooped up all day with only their feet to stare at. Imagine what it's like to be a pony, who, when in the wild, is used to being outdoors the whole time, with a far greater degree of freedom than you will ever be able to give your animal. Bear this fact in mind when you 'simply can't be bothered' or are 'way too tired' to give your pony a thorough working.

It's also worth remembering that your pony
will appreciate an occasional lazy day off
where they are just turned out in the field without
being ridden.

Horses and their riders have a right to ride on the roads, but you should only do so if you are a competent rider and are completely able to control your horse. Here are ten basic safety tips to help you stay out of danger. You should always follow these when riding on the road.

1. Walk or trot when riding on the roads. Never canter or gallop!

2. Ride with both hands on the reins, except when signalling.

3. Use the correct signals.

4. Avoid riding on the roads after dark or in poor visibility.

5. Wear fluorescent garments such as a hat cover,

body-warmer or tabard which are fitted with reflective strips. Fit the horse with similar high-visibility leg bands and stirrup torches.

6. Always ride on the appropriate side of the road to move with the flow of traffic.

7. Always ride in single file when riding in a group with the quietest horse at the front to set a good example for the following horses and riders.

8. Remember that it is an offence to ride on a pedestrian footpath.

9. In the UK, the law upholds your right to use a defined bridle path.

10. When a driver stops or slows for you, always acknowledge their consideration to encourage them to do it again next time they encounter a horse.

YAY or NEIGH

THINGS PONIES LOVE AND HATE

PONIES SAY YAY TO:

1. SUGAR CUBES
2. WATER
3. SOFT MUSIC
4. BEING PETTED
5. GROOMING
6. OTHER PONIES
7. FRESH, LUSCIOUS GRASS
8. EXERCISE
9. ROLLING AROUND IN THE MUD
10. CARROTS

PONIES SAY NEIGH TO:

1. MEAT
2. FIRE
3. LOUD NOISES
4. STRANGERS
5. SNAKES
6. FLAPPING CLOTHES
7. DECIDUOUS TREES

NEW LIFE

THE RSPCA RECOMMENDS THAT A HORSE OR
PONY'S HEAD COLLAR BE TAKEN OFF BEFORE IT
IS LEFT LOOSE AND UNSUPERVISED IN A FIELD.

On average, a mare's pregnancy lasts around 345 days. Towards the end, she will become restless and uncomfortable. If she were in the wild, expectant mum and foal would be prime targets for predators. She will appreciate peace and quiet at this time.

Signs that a mare is about to come 'in foal' include: sweating, pacing up and down, turning to look at or even kicking at her belly and pawing at the ground.

The mare will give birth under the cover of dark, when no-one is around.

The foal is born with open eyes and is normally able to stand up within an hour. After about 40 minutes, it starts to twist its ears around, reacting to sounds. Within hours, the foal can almost keep up with its mum, running around the fields and responding to the comforting 'nickering' sounds that she makes.

Within two hours the new-born foal has normally found its mother's breast, and is feeding off the all-important first milk, the colostrum. For at least the next nine months, the foal will feed off its mother's milk. Then it starts to eat grass.

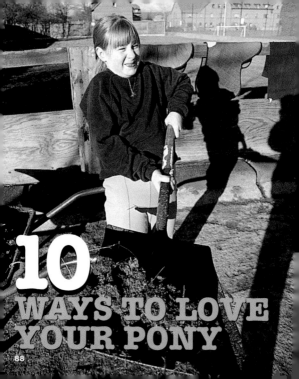

10
WAYS TO LOVE
YOUR PONY

All ponies need to be shown that they are loved by their owners. And every now and then your pony might deserve a special treat. Here are ten ways to show a pony you care:

1. Give your horse a special food treat to reward it for good behaviour. Try a healthy alternative to sugar cubes such as an apple or carrot.

2. Pat it and stroke it along the lie of the coat.

3. Give your horse a thorough groom.

4. Tell your horse how good and clever it is.

5. A horse might enjoy a splash in a stream on a warm summer's day.

6. Add extra bedding to its sleeping area if it is tired or cold.

7. Try exercising it with another horse. As horses are herd animals, they enjoy the company of others.

8. Try 'finger-nibbling' your pony's mane. Use your fingers to make little pinches up and down the length of its mane, as though you were another horse affectionately nibbling and grooming it.

9. A change is as good as a rest! Put your horse in a fresh paddock for a change of scenery.

10. Give your horse's stable or stall a special spring clean and a thorough mucking out to show your pony just how important it is to you.

FAVOURITE

The amount of TV programmes and films that have been made about ponies just goes to prove how popular they are. Here are our ten all-time favourites:

1. BLACK BEAUTY

2. NATIONAL VELVET

3. CHAMPION, THE WONDER HORSE

4. MISTER ED

5. THE HORSE WHISPERER

6. SILVER (FROM THE LONE RANGER)

7. HERCULES (FROM STEPTOE AND SON)

8. MY LITTLE PONY

9. PEGASUS (FROM HERCULES)

10. SYLVESTER

PONIES